The recipe to heal anxiety

By Amira Dawoud

Table of contents

Introduction

Hi, my friends. I need to start this book by explaining that I am not a doctor, nor a nurse, and have nothing to do with the medical field. I am writing this book to talk about my own experience with all the information that is given inside of it. This book was a result of many years of studying and testing. All the information inside it has been tested by therapists and people who work in the mental health field. The most exciting part about this book is that all the information included, I found out by myself by noticing the changes within my mind and body under all kinds of life stresses. I was able to notice the mental and physical changes that happened after I had my very first panic attack. Then, I was able to figure out the normal ways that could be done to help change the direction that I was going in. Luckily, I was able to talk to some therapists and some people who work in that field, which have their own way to solve and heal mental problems. I was able to figure everything out myself throughout my everyday noticing what was really going on within my mind and body in specific details. This book took me years to be done because I wanted to make sure that all the information that I am including inside is 100% effective. I did go through many ups and downs, I did go through very bad days that caused me to find even deeper information that I also included in this book to help you all when you are ready to take this journey into mental healing. Many downs that I went through were very tough on me, but with each hit, I was able to know what I didn't know before. This book is really precious, and it is the real conclusion to all you need to do by yourself to reach the point that you are mentally stable for the rest of your life. I wish you all the luck once you decide to commit to this journey that by doing it and by starting it, you'll be giving yourself the most precious gift that you need at that point in your life.

You have panic attack disorder and anxiety disorder. That is what my family doctor told me at his office when I visited him after feeling some changes in my body. Here is my story.

I was almost 30 years old, a mother of two little boys, one is three years old and the other is one year old. I considered myself a normal person, meaning I used to do my everyday work very normally, such as taking care of my kids, going to the gym, and doing household chores like cleaning and cooking. Basically, nights were my only rest time. I could shower and sleep like a dead body after a long day. So, this is how it really started.

One day, I was driving on the highway on a rainy day, and suddenly a car slipped in front of me, hit the wall, and pushed back toward my car. It was so close that I had to act fast to avoid it. Now here's the thing, I panicked. I was very scared and showered myself with all the fear that I have. Days went by after this incident until a few weeks later, I started to feel a little uncomfortable and scared while driving, especially in some streets and at some traffic lights. I continued like that for a few weeks, trying to ignore any fear or uncomfortable feeling by singing or talking to someone on the phone while driving or just simply driving.

At this time, I found a part-time job to support my family and to do a little thing as any mom that felt that her future was taken over by these little creatures that she brought into this life. It was very close to my house and it was a super easy job. I started it, and after working for a few weeks, things suddenly changed. One day I was driving to work when suddenly I felt as if something was choking me. I stopped the car on the side of the street, rested for a few minutes, and then continued to work. At work, I was feeling terribly uncomfortable, but I chose to continue my short shift. When it was time to leave, I got into my car to drive home but never could because I suddenly started crying and had to call my husband to pick me up. I was crying for no reason. Since that day, my whole life changed and took another level at which I was able to write this book that will help many people and will save many lives from fear and pain.

The truth is that none of these details really matter. Why? Because it's only my story that could be yours as well. No matter what the details or the situation, it is only life under stress. Why am I saying this? Because what was going before the incident is the truth about all of it. How I was living my life socially, financially, emotionally, and physically caused all of that to happen, but the car accident that I saw earlier was the trigger to what happened next. So now let me explain.

During the last five years of my life, I got married, moved from one small country to a big and busy one, left all my family and friends, had two boys, and struggled financially and socially. So basically, my life was a mess. I was really strong and did everything that should be done to make it work and continue working. I stood for myself and my family in all situations and made it through it all, which made me think that at this point, everything, including myself, is okay. But the truth is that everything was okay except for me. I was tired, unhappy, and overall stressed. At that point in my life, I didn't realize it until it was too late because I ended up having a panic attack.

So back to what happened the other day. When my husband picked me up and sent me home, I was going through some emotions that I never felt before in my entire life. I was able to know what fear is and how painful it can be when it takes over your body and mind. Fear of being alone, fear of taking a bath, fear of dying suddenly, and leaving my two kids alone. All of these painful thoughts came to me in one second, and I felt my brain as if it was being eaten by these thoughts and taking over any bright side of my life. Even looking at my little adorable kids, I couldn't see the beauty of it. All I was able to see is the mess they were causing in the house.

So a few days after this incident, I visited the doctor who explained to me that it is an anxiety and panic attack disorder that is happening to me, which means that I will always be afraid that the panic attack might possibly happen to my body at any time. That week was so hard that I couldn't do my normal duties, such as taking care of my kids and taking care of the house. I couldn't even take care of myself because I was so tired that I couldn't leave the bed.

At that point, I was taking some anxiety medicine which was prescribed by the doctor to me as the only solution to get well, and with time the medicine dose would be reduced until I became medicine-free. So as a person who knows nothing about anxiety, I took the medicine and followed the doctor's directions, thinking just like any person that medicine is the solution for any sickness. Unfortunately, the medicine made me feel like a zombie. I was a body walking and moving without any emotions, just like a dead body. It also affected my vision after taking it for one week. I was terrified, and I still remember the taste of adrenaline in my tongue when I wasn't able to see normally for a few seconds . Although it was that short time that my vision was very blurry, I still decided momentarily that I would totally stop this medicine, without realizing that I would end up paying a very high price for being medicine-free. So I fell into a depression trap, which was the hardest few days of my entire life. I ended up leaving my job, I was in my bed almost all day, I couldn't be with my kids, take care of them, or even feed them. I also couldn't take care of myself. I was losing weight daily. I did not talk to anyone and did not want to talk to anyone. Until after two weeks of being in that trap when I decided to change and get out of bed.

So here's the big question: What is a panic attack and how does it form?

A panic attack is a form of the body getting rid of all the negative emotions and energy that accumulate within the body and mind over time. This depends on the lifestyle and the way a person deals with situations in their life, as well as on family history and genes inherited from parents. It occurs with discomfort in the body, feeling like a shock that mostly causes the heart to beat strongly, body shaking, sweating (especially in the hands and feet), a feeling of choking or discomfort while breathing, dizziness, and pressure on the brain.

Some people, when experiencing a panic attack, may mistakenly believe they have issues with their heart or that something is wrong with their body, without realizing it's only a panic attack. Some may even think it's similar to a heart attack. Alongside these physical symptoms, there is a rush of negative thoughts that can make you feel as if you've lost control of your mind, leading to a sense of fear stemming from these negative thoughts.

In reality, nothing major is happening. Because your body is under heavy pressure from negative emotions, it forms a panic attack to release some of that energy when you aren't taking any physical or mental action to release it. Regardless of how many tests you may undergo to check what's wrong, the results will typically show as normal unless you have other diseases, which are essentially unrelated topics in this book.

A panic attack could literally happen to any one of us, no matter who we are. It's a reflection of how you think about all that is happening in your life. When I say "think," it's all about the thoughts you put in your mind that shapes the situation, whether positively or negatively. If you suggest in your mind that the situation is hard, bad, painful, not possible to be solved, or tough, then you'll likely deal with negative outcomes. On the other hand, if you approach it with a positive attitude, believing you will try your best or that it happened for your benefit, then you'll face a brighter future.

Now, you might wonder, "Will I end up having a panic attack at some point in my life no matter what?" The answer is no. If you're someone who tends to keep emotions inside and doesn't easily express them, you have a higher chance of experiencing one. On the other hand, if you're someone who expresses emotions easily, it might take longer or even never happen. We all go through difficulties, problems, or hard situations that we have to deal with. The way you choose to deal with the situation determines the result in your life. Choosing to deal with any situation means you have certain thoughts about it. If you take things easily and have a thought like "things will pass, and I will be able to accomplish things easily," then it will pass easily. But if you view these situations as 'big problems' and see them as "unsolvable," then things might linger and might never go away.

When a panic attack hits, it's a sign from the body that it is in tension, but you're not giving it attention.

You simply need to give your body and brain attention to what is going on. And this happens by just living it day by day. Forget the past and ignore the future. Focus just on those moments and words that you are reading. Focus on your body sensation while reading them. Focus on your breath, coming in and out of your body.

You might say, "Oh, it's easy to say focus on your present, life is so busy and tense, and there is a lot going on." This is all made up by you and only you because you choose to think about what you believe in. The easiest thing to do is to live in the present moment because we are all born in that nature. This is our instinct. But we kept talking and thinking of the bad stuff until we believed in them. We trained our bodies and minds to be in tension and stress all the time. We trained ourselves on this pattern until we believed that this is how things are going, and we even forgot to feel our bodies.

We are moving and going with our lives so fast until we leave no time for our body and mind. We shut it off completely. We don't want to hear it anymore. We don't want to listen anymore. Because you know what listening means – it means losing the next deal. Listening means, for example, leaving this hectic relationship, and we are afraid to do so. Listening means losing the next opportunity. Listening means not taking the next flight. Yes, listening means losing all of these things. And you are not willing to lose. You might be afraid, not confident enough, or think that you're not capable of doing so. You'd rather keep running and pushing until the last breath instead of listening to your body. You muted your body to the point that it hated you.

So I guess you know the rest. Your body hit you with a panic attack because you really deserve it. You did not listen. Your body was in tension, and you did not give it attention.

Fight or flight situation.

The panic attack puts the body in a phase called a fight or flight situation. This phase implies that the person having a panic attack is under some kind of danger that requires them to either fight and act fast or run away as fast as possible. When the body enters this phase, it needs to interact rapidly to respond. If the person decides to fight, the heart will pump as fast as possible, causing blood to rush into the arms and legs. Similarly, if the person decides to run, the heart will beat rapidly, directing blood to the arms and legs. In this situation, less blood will be in the less critical parts of the body, such as the brain and internal organs, leading to feelings of dizziness and stomach pain.

This is a normal phase that everyone must experience, but it is typically healthy and okay when there is a real danger. However, in the case of a panic attack, there is no actual danger. The body reacts the same way even when there is no danger. The person feels these body sensations and changes while standing or sitting in a normal situation, but they are not feeling calm. Experiencing these sensations can cause the person to panic more and be afraid of these abnormal feelings. This is where the panic attack disorder begins, characterized by the fear of having these body sensations repeatedly. Later on, I will teach you methods on how to deal with each situation to overcome anxiety permanently.

Why do some people have the panic attack disorder?

It depends on the amount of emotions each person shows and expresses at the moment of a panic attack, as well as on their lifestyle and the level of drama in their life.

For example, in my case, my panic attack happened while I was driving, so I thought it occurred because of a fear of driving. However, what makes it worse is the negative thoughts the person starts adding to the list. The more you think of it, the longer the list becomes. When the panic attack forms, it comes with a huge stream of negative thoughts, as I just mentioned, that truly requires strength and courage from the person to stop it right there and not let it grow. If these thoughts keep growing, they might end up becoming like a spiderweb, leading the person to withdraw from life and limit social interactions, avoiding gatherings or events, thinking they might pose a danger to someone suffering from anxiety and panic attack disorder. I will explain that later on.

The physical and mental symptoms

In this section of my book, I will talk about the physical and mental changes that will happen after a panic attack forms in someone's life. Some people will end up experiencing all these changes, while others will have some of them. The severity of each of these changes might also vary from one person to another. They might occur all together or one after another. But in general, these are the changes that I ended up experiencing and learning, so I can share them with you.

1. Diarrhea. Diarrhea is one of the strongest symptoms of anxiety and panic attacks due to the fear it generates within the body. It begins as a flame of pain in the stomach and digestive system, sometimes lasting for a few weeks or months until anxiety subsides.

2. Constipation. Constipation is another major symptom arising from the anger within the body during anxiety.

3. Skin and hair changes. All this occurs due to stress impacting the body, causing skin damage, blisters, premature aging, and hair loss. Stress hormones from anxiety lead to a fight or flight situation, directing blood away from less critical areas like the skin and hair, causing the skin to age faster and the hair cells to be weaker causing the hair loss.

4. Dizziness. Dizziness results from the fight or flight situation during anxiety, as blood prioritizes certain body parts, causing the oxygen levels to be imbalanced in the brain, which will cause dizziness.

5. Pain in the digestive system. This is a consequence of stress affecting internal parts, leading to diarrhea, constipation, or inflammation. There will be strong pain that can be felt as a flame in the internal area.

6. Insomnia. Insomnia is a strong and famous symptom of anxiety, causing sleeping problems. Even when the body is worn out, the person might sleep for a few hours or sometimes not at all.

7. Lack of energy. This is a result of excessive stress hormones depleting mental and physical energy throughout the day.

8. Changes in facial expressions. I call it the "depression look," reflecting the emotional toll of anxiety, as when a person is feeling anxious and stressed it all changes the facial expression of that person.

9. Loss of appetite and weight loss. It occurs due to the massive stress produced in the body, the pain in the digestive system will lead the individual to avoid food, as well as these stress hormones will lead to less appetite anyway.

10. The immune system shuts down. This happens naturally during stress, leaving the body more susceptible to illnesses.

11. Overall weakness. It results from the constant consumption of energy by stress hormones, leaving the person fatigued and unfocused.

12. Fear. Fear is a foundational factor in mental problems, causing the person to perceive everything with fear.

13. Loss of excitement and passion. This happens when anxiety drains the person's energy and doing things becomes hard and painful due to anxiety.

14. Jealousy. Jealousy can arise from low self-esteem caused by anxiety, leading to feelings of inadequacy. But keep in mind that it is an outcome to anxiety, and will melt away once anxiety is cured.

15. Limiting social activities. This stems from the fear of having another panic attack, resulting in anxiety disorders.

16. Guilt and shame. This emerges from feeling incapable of participating in enjoyable activities with loved ones, breaking down the person's confidence.

17. Mood swing. That is a very common change that occurs, and it happens throughout the hours of one day many times, from feeling good to having some low energy, or feeling happy to sad and depressed.

Depression

Depression is one important side effect that is closely connected to anxiety and a stressful lifestyle. It can be identified simply as the deficiency of happiness hormones in the human body to a certain level that will cause the individual to experience depression. When I mention a "certain level," I mean that the deficiency can occur without leading to depression, but when it reaches a specific level, depression occurs. While any normal person may go through days feeling a little down, it doesn't necessarily indicate depression. However, when depression hits, the happiness hormones are so low that the person feels down most of the time.

Some doctors believe that depression is caused by completely different factors. They observe that when a person rejects the past they had to go through, rejects the future regardless of its proximity, and also rejects the present moment, it can lead to depression. In such cases, individuals need to work on their mental health to address these feelings, often requiring the expertise of professionals in the field.

Regarding the hormonal issue, we can prevent this problem by increasing the levels of happiness hormones. The medication also follows a similar strategy. However, this process requires time, commitment, and continuity. After researching real cases of people who experienced depression, I concluded that it takes at least one to three months for a patient to start feeling progress after beginning depression medication. In my opinion, instead of relying solely on medication, we can explore normal and natural ways in our daily lives to combat depression.

I must emphasize that if someone is already on medication, they should not stop without consulting their doctor. It's essential to seek professional advice to ensure the right course of action. I am sharing the methods that have worked for me and many others, but each person is unique. Let's delve into these methods that can help prevent and limit depression in our lives.

1. Exercise is a natural way to increase happiness hormones. It can be done in any way that feels suitable, such as walking, dancing, group exercises, yoga, or any other form. The key is to reach the sweating point and feel that the exercise was sufficient, as the body needs to reach a certain point for happiness hormones to surge.

2. Healthy diet. Eating certain types of food can naturally boost happiness hormones. Examples include dark chocolate, salmon fish, fruits, vegetables, eggs, raw nuts, and healthy meats. While I'm not prescribing a specific diet, incorporating these foods into your meals can significantly contribute to feeling better and preventing depression.

3. Happy feelings. Smiling and maintaining a happy demeanor throughout the day can increase happiness hormones. Avoiding anything that induces sadness and instead engaging in activities like watching comic shows and movies can keep you in a positive state, preventing depression.

4. Meditation has been proven to prevent depression by releasing hormones that promote relaxation. It has positive effects on various aspects of the body and mind, making it one of the most effective ways to remove and prevent depression.

5. Limiting stress is crucial in preventing depression, as stress often leads to it. Embracing a lifestyle focused on relaxation and self-care can help individuals steer clear of depression.

Medication

I must emphasize that I am not a doctor and have no affiliation with any scientific agency. My perspective on medication is based solely on personal experience and extensive research. It's crucial to note that if you are currently undergoing medication or therapy, consulting your doctor before making any changes is essential.

Mental health medication aims to alleviate the symptoms of conditions like depression and anxiety. For depression, medication focuses on increasing happiness hormones until reaching a level where the individual feels better. However, it doesn't address the root cause of depression. Similarly, for anxiety, medication may numb the brain to halt overthinking about anxious thoughts but does not eliminate the underlying reasons for anxiety. In essence, medication is designed to manage or reduce symptoms rather than treat the core cause of mental health issues.

Many medications can make your body and brain seem robotic, carrying out tasks without genuine emotions or reactions. Finding the right medication often involves trying various options, each with potential side effects like dizziness, fatigue, lack of focus, sleepiness, or nausea. Patients may undergo a trial-and-error process, trying different medicines until they discover one that minimizes adverse effects.

Over time, some patients may find the initial benefits diminish, leading doctors to suggest stronger doses, potentially fostering dependence on the medication. It's an alarming cycle that prompts the realization that there must be a better way to address these issues.

I want to assure you that there are alternative and more effective approaches. Many individuals, including myself, have successfully navigated these challenges naturally. Healing your body and mind from within can lead to a different, more satisfactory outcome. Depression is not an inherent illness; it often stems from lifestyle, specific problems, or traumas. By addressing these root causes and fixing your body and mind, you can achieve lasting improvement. This same principle applies to anxiety – fixing your thinking, mind, brain, and body from within can yield a more positive outcome. This is the essence of the message behind this book.

Why does a panic attack keep repeating?

The fact that panic attacks keep continuing and appearing in somebody's life doesn't mean that there's something wrong with this person. When a panic attack happens for the first time, usually, this uncomfortable feeling scares the person who is having one. As I said before, most people don't realize what is going on with them, and as a result, they become very scared, refusing those emotions and body sensations they are experiencing. With them rejecting and refusing what is going on, they basically try to suppress it down, hide it, and not make it go away. Let me explain this point deeper so you can understand it completely.

A panic attack can be seen as a way the body tries to release accumulated negative energy to prevent potential illnesses. Although the experience can be terrifying, understanding that the body is working to eliminate this energy can help reduce fear. By accepting and calmly breathing through the sensations, the body can effectively release this energy and alleviate panic attacks. Viewing them as a gift rather than a frightening occurrence might help individuals cope better and ultimately prevent future health issues.

It's important to understand that accepting the discomfort of a panic attack doesn't guarantee that it will disappear forever. The body tends to follow familiar paths, like a ball sliding on a muddy path. If a panic attack occurred once, the body might find it easier to trigger another one in response to negative energy. However, finding healthy ways to release this energy, such as exercise, dancing, painting, or other activities you enjoy, can help prevent future panic attacks. It's about either accepting the possibility of panic attacks or proactively channeling the energy in a positive direction.

Now, after finding a way to release this energy, it's time to address the thoughts ingrained in your brain for years. Working on these thoughts is the most crucial part of the healing journey. Fixing your thoughts about the panic attack itself by accepting it and realizing it's not a beast leads to full healing. You can't live thinking you can deal with a panic attack, no matter how many times it happens, without addressing and changing those underlying thoughts. The goal is to reduce panic attacks and accept them, fostering healing.

When this entire Earth was created, there were signs illustrating how things happen. The volcano can be a great example of how the human body works. When the volcano has too much pressure inside, it tends to explode so that it can release everything happening inside out onto the surface, allowing it to calm down and be relieved. After exploding, the volcano is calm again. So, the Earth created a way to expel all of this energy through the volcano. The same concept applies to the human body, which has found a way to eliminate excess emotions, energy, and internal pressure through a bodily reaction that mental health doctors decided to name a panic attack.

Imagine if the Earth kept hiding and squeezing all the energy inside it. Picture a scenario with no volcanoes and no outlet for the Earth to release this surplus energy being generated within. In such a situation, the Earth might explode, but in that case, it would be irreversible. Similarly, if the human body has no way to expel this energy, it could result in significant internal damage as the body tries to release it.

Early signs that something is wrong

Signs that something is wrong arise when you start taking aspects of your life too seriously. I want to clarify that I'm not suggesting you joke about your life, but when your reactions to events become intense, it's worth reconsidering. For instance, if your kids make too much noise and you respond with a lecture on behavior, or if your spouse is slightly late, causing your entire mood to change, these reactions indicate a need for reflection. Even a missed return call or a long grocery store line leading to annoyance suggests a deeper issue.

Life inherently presents challenges, without a predictable daily trajectory. How we perceive and engage with each day and its events defines our character—whether we are calm or anxious, angry or happy. Approach things with ease, and observe how your mood and overall life transform, influencing those around you. Changing your attitude alters the way you label events. A negative attitude may brand a grocery store line as a "waste of time" or "pain in my feet," while a positive attitude sees it as an opportunity to gather necessities or prepare a great meal.

Now, I pose a question for your thoughtful consideration.

Have you ever experienced a situation that was supposed to be very normal, like receiving a phone call or visiting a friend, yet you felt your heart beating fast, struggled to breathe, or experienced adrenaline rushes in your mouth and body?

If yes, I am telling you, please work on yourself, because what really happens is that if you are facing a problem, dealing with a challenging situation, or interacting with people you don't like but have to deal with, every time you handle it improperly, you add more pressure on your body and brain. This pressure is essentially stress. Every time you go through some form of stress, no matter how short it is, your body releases stress hormones. Once you relax, the stress hormones will return to normal levels in your body, but the more stressful life you are living, the more stress hormones rush through your body.

Now, imagine those hormones going up and down very frequently. However, in this situation, the stress hormones will go up and reach the red line, causing them to take longer and requiring more work to return to normal, because your body reached a point where your brain thinks that the rush of stress hormones is the normal state it needs to maintain. The body may tend to produce stress hormones sometimes even if you are not under any real stress or tension, leading to anxiety, where stress hormone levels are high even when no real stress is present. But what is truly behind it all is your predominantly negative thought patterns, even in normal situations.

Anxiety

Anxiety is a way of living in which a person is in constant worry and over thinks about the future. They tend to view situations negatively, even everyday occurrences. In their mind, every happening is perceived as a potential danger, regardless of how normal it may seem to others. Unfortunately, this mindset is not a joke for those who suffer from anxiety. They take things very seriously and are strongly convinced about their thoughts.

Anxiety doesn't emerge out of nowhere; it develops due to prolonged periods of a stressful life and various pressures, often stemming from relationships. Traumas, which I'm not discussing in my book, also contribute to the development of anxiety.

Anxiety can arise from various sources, but it's crucial to understand that you play a significant role in allowing anxiety to manifest. I'm not here to blame or break you down; rather, I want to emphasize that you are the one responsible for your life. Taking responsibility means being accountable for your actions, reactions, and thoughts, influencing your behavior.

When faced with a situation, different people respond differently. Some view it as challenging or problematic, while others see it as normal. Your initial perspective and attitude toward the situation set the stage for the outcomes. You can either ignite the fire by becoming nervous, stressed, anxious, moody, sad, or angry, leading to unfavorable results. On the contrary, adopting a neutral perspective allows for solutions to emerge. Viewing the situation as part of everyday life promotes smooth progress, devoid of negative energy and emotions.

Anxiety—this word, filled with fear and negativity, may surprise you when you realize the number of people living with it daily. You might feel a deep sympathy for those experiencing the unfairness of life, and suddenly find yourself among them. Upon reflection, you'll see that anxiety contributes significantly to stress in someone's life. Initially, it may seem that stress stems only from work, finances, relationships, world events, or a lifestyle dominated by fear. However, delving into each area reveals hidden reasons and underlying causes for the anxiety. If a person is anxious about work, there must be a concealed reason behind it. Similarly, if someone frets about finances and money, there should be an underlying cause. Moreover, if someone experiences anxiety in relationships, there must be a genuine hidden reason for that.

Digging into the roots of anxiety and its causative factors, I've identified key elements that contribute to this mental state. Prior to the onset of anxiety, certain signs and emotions emerge in an individual's life, signaling a potential journey toward anxiety as a problem. In my perspective, relationships stand out as one of the primary catalysts that can lead a person into the clutches of anxiety. However, it is crucial to recognize specific cracks and issues within these relationships that give rise to anxiety.

One prevalent form of relationship-induced anxiety is separation anxiety. This type of anxiety can manifest in various situations involving separation, with the separation being profound on a soul level. Those prone to this type of anxiety experience a deep mental disconnect, feeling the impact once physical separation occurs. An example is a mother being separated from her children, often stemming from divorce or relationship breakdown. Additionally, separation may occur when a mother has work-related obligations, causing mental distress. In such cases, readiness to confront and manage anxiety becomes paramount for both the mother and the children.

Another scenario that may trigger anxiety is when a child gets married, with the emotional impact primarily affecting the mother or father, but predominantly the mother. It's essential to note that not all cases are uniform, as individual readiness to cope with anxiety varies based on personality and mental health.

Another form of relationship-induced anxiety is trapping anxiety, which can manifest in various types of relationships beyond marriage or romantic entanglements. It extends to familial connections or any relationship where one person's behavior causes anxiety in the other. This dynamic can occur between parents and children, with one or both parents exerting excessive control, leading the children to feel trapped.

As with other forms of anxiety, mental preparedness plays a crucial role in how individuals navigate these situations. Some individuals possess the strength and diverse personalities that enable them to resist succumbing to anxiety. In such cases, rather than experiencing anxiety, these individuals may emerge stronger and more resilient, potentially carving out a path toward leadership or positions of power as they navigate through challenging relationships.

Another form of relationship-induced anxiety, which I label "lack of safety anxiety," can arise in various types of relationships—whether within family dynamics, marriage, or romantic connections. As the name implies, this anxiety occurs when one member of the relationship experiences a sense of insecurity or lack of safety in their dealings with the other person. Such feelings often stem from the actions of the member causing the anxiety, displaying selfishness and a lack of care or compassion towards their partner. This mistreatment can induce high levels of anxiety in the individual who feels unsafe within the relationship.

Another prevalent type of anxiety, which I refer to as "lack of love anxiety," spans across various relationships, whether in the realms of love, romance, family, or others. This potent form of anxiety profoundly impacts individuals, manifesting when a person feels they are not receiving sufficient love from those around them, particularly from someone crucial in their life. In romantic relationships or marriages, if one partner consistently fails to express love, it can lead to feelings of self-doubt and low self-esteem, ultimately culminating in anxiety.

Similarly, within familial connections, the repercussions of parents not providing ample love, whether intentionally or unintentionally, can be distressing for a child. The child may develop a sense of being surplus or unnecessary within the family, causing discomfort and adversely affecting self-confidence and mood, particularly during their early years. The lack of love extends its impact across various aspects of the child's life, contributing to a sense of falling apart.

In dealing with a challenging person, such as a demanding boss, the choice to be anxious or not lies within your control. For instance, if your boss assigns tasks outside your job scope or treats you in a way you find unpleasant, expressing your boundaries directly can help alleviate anxiety. Politely stating, "This is not part of my job" or expressing your desire to be treated fairly can set clear expectations.

Rather than dwelling on negative thoughts or venting to colleagues, directly addressing the issue with your boss is the most straightforward way to maintain an anxiety-free approach. While it may not be easy, it allows you to communicate your feelings, needs, and boundaries. The outcome, whether acceptance or potential consequences, rests with your boss. If your concerns are acknowledged, it can eliminate negative feelings. If not, it might lead to job loss or worsened treatment, but standing up for yourself can boost confidence and self-pride, paving the way for future opportunities. Ultimately, the decision lies with you to choose a path either filled with anxiety or one that is anxiety-free, accepting the potential outcomes that may follow.

Here, I provided an example of dealing with a boss, but you will encounter various types of people. Some of them are family members, with whom you must continue dealing even when it feels challenging. It's crucial to be clear about how they treat you and express your preferences in relation to them.

For instance, if a sister or brother forces you to do something you don't want, you don't have to hide your negative emotions. Politely and clearly tell them that it's not something you're comfortable with and don't wish to continue. Whether they accept it or not is up to them, and it doesn't make you a bad person; it simply reflects different perspectives.

Expressing your desires and boundaries helps avoid harboring anxious thoughts or negative feelings. It's best to address such situations directly when they arise, calmly and honestly. You don't have to overthink it; act promptly and communicate what you want and don't want.

Each person is unique, with different needs and preferences. You shouldn't feel obligated to conform to others' expectations. Suppressing your true self to please others is a key contributor to anxiety. Making small adjustments is acceptable, but fundamentally changing who you are isn't healthy or beneficial.

Don't lose yourself in an attempt to fit in or please others. Being kind to people is essential, but sacrificing your true self is not. It only serves the happiness of others and their desire for you to conform. Strive for a balance that preserves your authenticity and mental well-being. Each and every one of us has our own fears, but we believe that we are old enough to have them. So, we hide them within and never admit to having them. The truth is, they are real and alive within us, but we keep hiding them deep, deep inside and not admitting to them. Eventually, these fears will come to the surface. There will be some situation, events, or even a type of lifestyle that will bring these fears to the surface and awaken them again. Examples include the death of a loved one, any kind of trauma, or worrying about something, such as your job, failing in school, or business. I'm talking about overthinking.

So, no matter what your fear is, it will come to life in a situation that matches that fear within you. For instance, if you fear failure, failing in any aspect of your life, such as school, business, marriage, or job, will bring this fear to the surface. You will start experiencing and testing these feelings and emotions. You might never know you have that fear until you go through it. Once you start feeling that fear, you have to work it out of your life as fast as possible because the longer it stays, the wider and stronger it will become. This fear of failure will start spreading into other areas of your life, taking all it can to grow. The mechanism of all fears is exactly the same – they consume all your positivity to grow and surround the body, building themselves up. Any positive thoughts or behaviors you already have inside your brain are attacked, eaten up, and replaced with a black, darkened space that can only be filled with nonsensical thoughts and behaviors that work against you.

Not only that, but when these fears surface, they directly impact human confidence, creating a slightly small crack in it. This crack can easily grow with every instance of rethinking and acting upon that fear. This occurs when you start incorporating this fear into your life as if it is a normal way to live. We were never made from fear; we were born brave, confident, and ready to face it all. However, with life experiences, we came to believe that fear is the master of us all.

Anxiety comes and hits with a very big wave, destroying anything that stands in front of it, leaving damaged and shattered land behind. However, the difference between anxiety waves and tsunami waves is that anxiety waves were formed because of you. You kept blowing and blowing each time you saw it, acting from a negative perspective. You did it for a very long time, having enough power to form these anxious waves.

But you know what? Even after the tsunami, the city is rebuilt, and the same can happen with you. So, all you need to ensure is that when you rebuild yourself, do it even better and more beautifully. Make yourself shine from the inside out. Don't just rebuild; be creative and build yourself again because when anxiety comes, it wants you to become the best person you were born to be. It says, "This is your next step to shining, your next step to what you are here for." Take this step for a new beginning because I assure you, something magnificent is waiting for you. You are about to become a greater version of yourself, and no one can stop you.

Taking this first step, as easy as it seems on this paper you are reading, is the hardest. It requires all the power, courage, commitment, and the ability to listen to what is inside causing all this pain. What is wrong with you? What is happening inside your soul? Why did you reach this level of pain? Listen until it all comes out. No matter how long you've been running away, there will be a moment when you have to sit down and listen to yourself. Your self is in pain, tired, and not okay.

We essentially choose our fears

For someone with anxiety or panic attack disorder, avoiding various places becomes a common response. Places like grocery stores, social gatherings, and public spaces may be perceived as potentially dangerous, leading the person to believe that their house is the only safe place. In essence, the individual has chosen the house as their only fear-free haven. However, the power of choice lies within, and the thoughts a person chooses to cultivate shape their reality.

If the person decides to view other places as safe, expanding their comfort zone, a broader sense of safety can be established. Even for those with severe panic attack disorder, introducing new safe places can be a transformative process. For instance, encouraging the idea that the neighborhood is a safe place to walk can initiate positive change.

The key is repetition and belief. The chosen thought, such as "The neighborhood is a safe place, and I can walk in my neighborhood safely and happily," should be repeated until the brain internalizes it as a fact. Patience is crucial, especially when doubts arise. Even on difficult days, refrain from dismissing the idea; instead, affirm its truth.

Timing varies for each individual, influenced by personal circumstances, personality, and mental resilience. Consistency in reinforcing positive thoughts is vital. Be cautious not to counteract progress with contradictory statements. Mindfulness about self-talk and persistent commitment to positive affirmations contribute to lasting change.

Ultimately, the choice to remain trapped in fear or break free rests in your hands. Embrace new thoughts and ideas that serve your well-being and future. Despite the initial skepticism, these simple shifts in mindset can be transformative. Take the step; you have nothing more to lose, and everything to gain. Choose thoughts that empower and redefine your life.

Indeed, some individuals possess greater courage and a stronger will to change, enabling them to take significant steps. Rather than incrementally adding one step at a time, these individuals can boldly declare, "I am free wherever, I can go no matter where this place is and no matter what time it is in the day." This reflects a powerful mindset that transcends limitations.

The magnitude of one's thoughts directly influences their performance in life. Limiting thoughts restrict the steps one takes, whereas expansive thoughts result in broader and more impactful strides. The key lies in commitment and courage. Practicing and reinforcing positive thoughts contribute to faster and more substantial results in life. The more dedicatedly a person integrates these thoughts into their mindset, the more profound the positive changes become.

Most individuals experiencing panic attacks often designate their homes as a safe haven, where the threat of a panic attack seems less imminent. However, it's crucial to recognize that this perception is a decision they've made. By choosing to see their house as a safe zone, they have the power to make different decisions and cultivate thoughts that serve their well-being.

For example, affirmations like "I am safe everywhere and anywhere. I am safe inside and outside my home. I am safe alone and around other people" can be transformative. To set these phrases in motion, a conscious decision must be made.

As emphasized earlier, the key is making a decision. These decisions act as the fuel propelling the vehicle of change forward. To make these decisions, all you need to do is choose the ones that align with your well-being and benefit.

Your fears changed who you are

Your fears have altered who you are. It's essential to introspect deeply into your behaviors, especially when dealing with anxiety or panic attack disorders over an extended period. The changed behaviors often become a lifestyle, influenced by the fears that have taken root. To reclaim control over your life, you must consciously address and rectify each fear-driven thought.

While it may initially seem overwhelming, the process doesn't take as long as you might fear. As someone controlled by fear, you've likely generalized these thoughts to every aspect of your life. The key is to reverse this generalization without fear.

For instance, if the fear led you to decide that grocery shopping is too difficult, and you started buying everything online to avoid potential panic attacks in the store, you can break this pattern. Just tell yourself, "I don't need to shop online. I can go to the store confidently, without fearing a panic attack." Although it may require some practice, you'll be astonished at how quickly it can work. Stay conscious of your actions, reassure yourself that you no longer need to be afraid, and affirm your ability to do things normally.

Initiate this process with thoughts like, "I don't need to shop online," "Who said I have to be afraid?" and "I can go to the grocery store, have fun, shop everything I want, and return home safely." Over time, as you consistently practice these affirmations, you'll witness them spreading to every aspect of your life. The power lies in taking that first step and consciously challenging the fears that have shaped your actions.

Another example is when you are about to visit or have some kind of social event, and you are afraid because you're used to being anxious.

All you need to do is sit by yourself and think, 'why do I have to be anxious? Am I anxious because I don't want to have a panic attack in front of them?' But I've already explained to myself that I'm not going to have a panic attack. Why do I have to fear it anymore? I can be in this event, be with my family and friends, have fun, enjoy my life, and everything will be okay. All you need to do is practice these new thoughts and ideas to yourself, and you will be amazed at how effective and how quickly they work.

You've been dealing with these thoughts and behaviors for so long that you believed they were facts. However, the truth is, these thoughts and behaviors are not your facts; they are the result of you avoiding and running away from your fears. They've been present for so long that you thought you'd been like that forever.

Another idea is that every time you want to drive a car on the highway, for example, you feel anxious. You've become accustomed to being afraid and worried, spending too many years in this anxious state even when there's nothing to worry about. To address this, practice being conscious again about why you're anxious. Ask yourself, 'Why am I anxious? Can I drive? Am I a good driver? Am I afraid of having an accident, or is it the fear of another panic attack in the car?' Remind yourself that you know how to handle stress and assure yourself that you won't have a panic attack because you know how to release stress from your body. You can enjoy driving to your destination, have fun, and return safely. Repeat these thoughts to yourself consistently, and over time, generalize them to various aspects of your life, just as you practiced fear until it generalized to everything. It might take a few days to feel the difference in everything you do, so keep practicing. You have nothing to lose, so give it a try for a change and relief in your life.

Emotions

Emotions play a crucial role in maintaining overall health. To achieve a healthy state from within, both your body and brain cells should thrive. Unhealthy emotions like sadness, fear, hatred, shame, and guilt can be detrimental to the human mind. The longer these emotions linger within the body, the more harm they inflict, and the intensity of these emotions accelerates the damage. Initially, this damage may manifest as occasional headaches or fleeting pain, but if ignored, it can escalate into a full-fledged illness. Each emotion tends to impact a specific organ, and complete healing often requires the release of these emotions. Physical ailments or pain serve as clear signals from the body, indicating an imbalance in emotions and thoughts. Understanding these cues is essential for addressing the root cause. Cultivating positive emotions and vibes contributes to better health, acting as a magnet for emotions like love, happiness, and forgiveness.

Releasing emotions

Consider this analogy: envision a smoothly flowing highway with normal traffic until an unexpected accident causes congestion and blockages. The highway remains paralyzed until emergency services arrive to clear the wreckage. Similarly, emotional blockages can occur within your body due to trauma, pain, anger, or other negative emotions. Releasing these emotions is akin to removing the blockage, allowing you to respond naturally to life events. If left unresolved, emotions like anger can persist and cause ongoing damage until addressed.

Newborns typically only possess innate fears of loud sounds and falling, with other fears acquired from their surroundings. As the brain learns these fears, individuals can actively replace them with healthier behaviors. While there's no predetermined time frame for specific illnesses, negative emotions can impact cellular health. Emotions such as shame, guilt, hatred, anxiety, or fear can manifest in various body parts, leading to illness based on their intensity and duration. Prolonged exposure to anxious or fearful situations can compromise the immune system, resulting in hormonal imbalances that contribute to bodily damage.

Extensive studies identify connections between certain emotions and potential illnesses, such as fear being linked to kidney damage. However, it's crucial not to dwell on specific associations to avoid creating unnecessary concerns. The key lies in recognizing that these emotional impacts can be healed and cured through a personal decision to release them. This involves changing your thoughts, subsequently altering your attitude toward these emotions.

Anger

You have to keep important information in your mind. Negative feelings will only lead to negative conclusions, no matter what the conclusions are: illness, sickness, strained relations, struggling. Some negative emotions can be much stronger and lead to faster damage in a person's life. One of these emotions is anger. Anger works strongly and deeply, going within the person's body and damaging almost anything. It stops the person's ability to see any bright side of life. Anger digs so deep that it brings with it most of the strong negative emotions, such as hatred. It locks the heart from receiving any good vibes or feelings from any situation, as well as blocking it from giving. And here, problems begin.

When this cycle of giving and receiving stops or has blockages, you will start noticing problems and issues rising in your life. It will start by showing signs in your daily life. For example, you will wake up feeling not okay, your mood will be low, you will have tension more often, and your reaction toward any situation, no matter how big or small, will be more than needed. Usually, people don't notice the signs. But now you should start to do so since you are reading and getting educated about it. Ignoring the signs will lead to bigger hits.

Now, I know that you are wondering, "But I'm a human being, can't I have emotions? Can I feel it? Can I have all kinds of emotions?"

Of course, you can and you will. So, let's learn some healthy ways and tips to release that anger, so it won't harm you. All you need to do is get this anger out of your body, and things will shift for the best. First, you must find someone who you can trust and just talk. But keep in mind that once you have talked the first time, don't talk about it again or overthink. Just talk to release, no more. Second, exercise. Yes, jump, run, dance, or do some activity that involves the whole body shaking to get rid of this energy. Third, shout, shout as loud as you can. Fourth, break a glass, just as simple as that. You can use your own imagination to release the anger but without harming yourself or others. You can do any of these ways by taking that decision that you're releasing this energy, not just increasing it or increasing its heavy load on you.

Breakdowns

Sometimes, after trying and working on yourself for a long time, you will make significant progress in your healing process. You will start to feel better and do better. Eventually, you are going to say it loud to yourself. Suddenly, a tough situation will show up with all of its power and pressure, causing you to feel like you did not go anywhere. Here, you might start thinking that all you have accomplished has evaporated. But that is not true. All the steps you took did count, and each step ahead is completely solid; there are no backward steps. All you have to do is accept the situation as it is, deal with it, and try your best to calm your emotions down. The situation will pass fast, and you will go back to the last step to continue progressing. This doesn't mean that tough situations are a must or meant to happen; it's just to show you that they might come, and you should never stop progressing.

In this section, I need to explain why, when those emotions are released in the body, they manifest as feelings of fear.

Now, let's learn a little bit about fear. Fear is one of the strongest and worst emotions that can be locked down in the human body. Fear digs so deep inside the body that it literally damages human cells. The more this fear stays within the body, the more damage it does. The stronger your fear is, the more damage it will cause. So, you have to keep in mind that the first thing that should be done is to release this fear as soon as possible with all the power you have, so you can save yourself from the possibilities of having a great illness.

You know, fear is fear. The human brain does not separate the fear of insects from the fear of driving, for example, or differentiate between the fear of heights and the fear of losing money in the future. The human mind deals with all types of fear in the same way, regardless of their differences or intensity. Let's take the example of someone fearing insects due to perceived dangers, such as potential pain, stinging, or venom. In this case, the brain categorizes it as a fear, and this fear becomes ingrained in the body.

Similarly, another person might fear losing money or becoming financially unstable. The brain acknowledges this as another fear. The more a person dwells on, thinks about, and takes actions based on these fears, the more intense the fears become. For instance, in the case of the fear of insects, if a person initially fears touching them, it may escalate to avoiding seeing or hearing them, amplifying the fear. With prolonged focus and emotional investment, the fear might evolve into a phobia, the most potent form of fear.

As individuals grapple with various fears and phobias, the cumulative impact results in internal distress and discomfort. Some may fear insects, losing money, aging, traveling, or various other aspects, creating a cycle of increasing fear interconnected with other stressors, leading to pressure within the body. Stress, acting as a pressure pot, compels the body to a breaking point, pushing all these fears to the surface. Individuals experiencing stress may either confront and manage these fears or risk the body responding with a panic attack.

While many people face stress and pressure, some effectively cope through regular exercise, engaging in physical activities, practicing meditation, or expressing emotions through activities like crying. Individuals unknowingly adopt strategies that help alleviate stress and prevent panic attacks.

Returning to the initial point, fear is a pervasive and potent emotion, deeply ingrained in human experience. As the body seeks to release negative energy, it prioritizes the release of fear, the most powerful and intense emotion. Every person on Earth harbors some fear, as we were raised and educated, often from infancy, with an introduction to fear. For instance, parents cautioning their children against potential harm is a common example. While these learned responses are natural, it is crucial to recognize and modify thought patterns and communication styles. Understanding that panic attacks are a means for the body to release emotions, especially fear, prompts individuals to work on themselves and their emotional well-being over time.

After experiencing the first panic attack, many people develop a fear of dying. It's a common fear that surfaces at various points in our lives, influenced by movies, shows, or stories of death that evoke worry and sadness. The sensations the body experiences during a panic attack mimic those of death, leading individuals to believe that they are dying, triggering the fear response in the brain.

However, the body's actions during a panic attack are a natural response to release pent-up negative emotions, relieving the body from a painful state. As mentioned earlier, likening it to a volcano eruption, the body shakes until it releases, and similarly, once we accept these emotions without fear, things will stabilize.

Yet, acceptance doesn't come easily for most people. The fear of these sensations often translates into a fear of death, creating a cycle where the fear intensifies, making it more challenging to let go. The rejection within us worsens the situation, amplifying the fear and prolonging its presence in the body. Breaking this cycle requires acknowledging and accepting these sensations rather than fearing them, ultimately leading to a healthier emotional state.

As mentioned earlier, the panic attack serves as a mechanism for the body to expel negative emotions. Given that fear is one of the most potent and challenging negative emotions that can overwhelm the human body and mind, the panic attack manifests when the body attempts to release this intense emotion. The body seeks to expel the emotion with the greatest impact, which, in this case, is fear, hence the term "panic attack." Many individuals may not immediately recognize that the underlying negative energy within their minds is rooted in fear, and this lack of awareness is entirely normal.

In the case of someone feeling unhappy about their financial situation, they might express thoughts and words like, "I'm not happy about my financial situation; I feel like I won't be able to pay my bills much longer than this time. If I stay in this space or in this way, I won't be able to make it." The underlying meaning of "I won't be able to make it" is essentially expressing fear—fear of not being able to continue, fear of not being able to improve the situation, and fear of facing more trouble. This fear becomes a repetitive loop in the person's mind.

Similarly, in relationships, if someone says, "I don't think this person is treating me well, or I'm not feeling really happy in my relationship, or my spouse is not treating me well," it reflects a fear. This person is afraid that if things remain unchanged, the relationship won't progress as desired. There's a fear of an impending end to the relationship, and a fear that satisfaction won't be achieved with the way the spouse is treating them. In essence, it's another manifestation of fear circulating in the individual's thoughts.

As these fears grow and loop in someone's mind, they deeply embed themselves. If the person is living a lifestyle that doesn't facilitate the release of these emotions, the body ultimately takes action to restore a sense of smoothness and relaxation.

The body forms this attack or mechanism to release these pent-up emotions, seeking to return to its natural state of relaxation. Anxiety, fear, and stress are not the norm; they are temporary states that, ideally, shouldn't serve as the natural baseline for the human body. The body is inherently designed to be in a relaxed form, and these emotional responses are more of a deviation from that natural state. Recognizing this and actively working to release these emotions is crucial for maintaining overall well-being.

Strong healing tools

Acceptance

When a person experiences a mental challenge, the brain typically operates with a continuous flow of thoughts. In such cases, the individual often endeavors to suppress these thoughts, initiating a struggle and internal conflict. The more one attempts to halt these thoughts, the more they tend to intensify.

So, what should you do, and how should you act? Begin by relaxing through deep breathing. Then, acknowledge and accept what is transpiring within you. Recognize that the internal processes are attempting to convey a message for your benefit and assistance. Accept the reality that these thoughts or feelings require time to articulate their message. Deal with your thoughts and emotions as you would with a baby attempting to communicate why they are crying. Just as you can't force a baby to stop crying, similarly, you must allow your thoughts and emotions the time they need to express and explain themselves.

Listen to them attentively until they have fully conveyed their message. Negative thoughts racing through your mind and the surge of negative emotions within your body necessitate time to settle and articulate what is wrong. The key difference is that a baby tends to communicate directly after calming down, whereas thoughts and emotions might take some time to be fully understood. The more you can accept, the easier it becomes to comprehend and relax. This is where you can progress in the healing process.

Acceptance entails embracing all the emotions, thoughts, and the situation causing pain. Once you fully accept these aspects, solutions will emerge, and the healing process will commence.

Embrace both mental and physical symptoms on your body and in your brain. Acceptance, in this context, means acknowledging all bodily symptoms, no matter how challenging or painful. During a panic attack, fearing the symptoms exacerbates the situation, leading to more rejection in the mind and intensifying symptoms. Practicing acceptance involves consciously relaxing and reassuring yourself that it's okay, these are temporary body symptoms that will eventually fade. Though challenging, understanding that a panic attack won't be fatal allows the brain to calm down.

While some may possess the mental strength to control a panic attack immediately, others may need to practice acceptance multiple times. When symptoms arise, find a comfortable place to sit or lie down, relax your muscles, and focus on controlled breathing. Acknowledge the sensations, reminding yourself they are temporary and will dissipate. You can even address the panic attack directly, expressing understanding and allowing it to pass through your body with ease. Speaking to it with compassion reduces hatred towards its effects, gradually increasing acceptance until it fades away.

Becoming proficient in accepting both physical and mental symptoms eliminates panic attacks. As you master acceptance, you'll observe panic attacks vanishing from your life because they served their purpose and are no longer necessary. This newfound freedom allows you to navigate life without the anticipation of the next panic attack, fostering a sense of liberation within yourself. By completely accepting that these sensations may arise anytime, anywhere, you can move forward in your life, pursuing your dreams and happiness with confidence. Simply take the step of acceptance and witness a transformative shift toward your best life.

I will now share a fact that can make acceptance much easier. The person must experience great pleasure when a panic attack occurs within the body. I say this with complete confidence, realizing it may be shocking for you to read these words. I express this because when the body takes action by forming a panic attack, it is essentially saving itself from potential serious illness if these negative energies linger for too long. The body, in its wisdom, decides to release these pent-up negative energies, saying, "That's enough of feeling them; I need to get them away from me."

When the body takes this action, it's crucial for the individual to recognize that their body is functioning perfectly well, at full capacity and with optimal health. The body made a necessary decision and executed it by forming a panic attack to prevent the development of illness. Therefore, the person should feel thrilled and happy that their body is working seamlessly.

This is the truth I'm sharing with you, and while it may be shocking, it is essential to acknowledge. It's important to reward your body by expressing gratitude for forming the panic attack within your body. Thank your body and convey your happiness that it is sending a message about the need to release accumulated negative energy. Always express gratitude to your body for successfully performing its job in the best way possible, maintaining your overall well-being. Be thankful to your body for saving you from potential serious illness if the panic attack hadn't occurred. After understanding this, who wouldn't be happy?

I understand that the sensations during a panic attack may not be pleasant, but embracing the fact that it's happening for the best can transform the experience. When you smile and feel happiness within yourself during a panic attack, it tends to subside faster, releasing built-up energy. Try this practice of smiling and being thrilled about your body's response to a panic attack. Anticipate the next one, express gratitude, and acknowledge that your body is working at its best to keep you healthy. By changing your perspective to one of power, love, and acceptance, you can shift your entire attitude toward panic attacks. This change in mindset fosters trust in your body's capabilities, replacing fear with confidence. Embrace this new outlook, and you'll notice a positive transformation in yourself, your body's reactions, and your thoughts, ultimately dissolving the rejection of your situation. Read and internalize this information to guide your life positively, accepting and understanding your situation instead of rejecting it.

Unconditional love

We, as human beings, are born with a natural inclination to love everything around us. We are designed to embrace love in every occurrence. Additionally, we are inherently meant to love ourselves. If you've ever observed a baby, you might notice how affectionately they gaze at each part of their body—the fingers, hands, feet, and toes. Babies often display self-love by kissing themselves or laughing when they see their reflection in the mirror. This innate love is an integral part of our nature from the very beginning.

However, as we grow older, external influences begin shaping our perspectives. Unfortunately, much of this input tends to be negative. For instance, as girls go through adolescence and their bodies undergo changes, many parents start advising them on dietary restrictions or cautioning against gaining weight. This information subtly conveys messages like "you're not good enough" or "you don't look as good as you should." This planted negativity can lead these children to develop self-hatred, particularly towards their bodies.

This example is just one among hundreds or even thousands of seeds planted in children's minds from the start, teaching them to harbor feelings of hatred, dislike, and anger. Rather than appreciating the incredible possibilities and abilities inherent in their beings, these children learn to despise themselves. This negativity continues to grow and manifests in various forms throughout their lives. As these children mature into adults, they may believe they understand everything correctly. However, life's challenges will eventually force them to confront situations that compel them to search within for the love that was lost at some point in their lives.

We all experience circumstances in life that diminish the love within us. Many situations lead us to judge and accuse others of causing the pain we endure. Ironically, the more we blame and charge, the more limited love becomes in our lives. The truth is, love has the power to heal us from all the pain within our lives.

As infants, we are born with an innate capacity to feel love for everything and everyone around us. This is evident in the robust and healthy growth of a baby's body and its rapid healing capabilities, fueled by pure love. It is this absence of love in our lives as adults that often leads to lingering injuries and prolonged pain. Numerous studies support the idea that love has the genuine ability to heal every form of pain.

In essence, the key takeaway is to integrate love into our lives consciously. By practicing love and nurturing it within our souls, we pave the way for internal healing.

Unconditional love serves as the key to unlocking doors and freeing oneself from anxiety and various mental issues. When faced with challenging situations, a person uttering the phrase "I can't take it anymore" is essentially expressing an inability to love the situation, the person causing the hardship, or the current location linked to the difficulty. As this individual dwells on the details and potential causes of the situation, the circle of not being able to love expands, surrounding them and exacerbating the challenges. Choosing not to love becomes a catalyst for mental issues.

Contrary to common belief, the opposite of love is not hate but rather fear. While hate is a partial counterpart, it finds expression through fear. If there is fear in any aspect of your life, it indicates the presence of something or someone you don't love. Adding judgment to this situation worsens matters. Judging places you in a position of superiority, asserting that you are a higher soul and better than the person or thing being judged.

Now, I have a few questions to ask you. Please answer truthfully, think, and take your time.

Do you love the people that you live with?

Do you love the people in your social circle?

Do you love your family?

Do you love the people you work with?

Do you love your job?

Do you love the house you live in?

Do you love the car that you have?

Do you love your neighbors?

And finally, do you love the person you are today?

I don't want to delve deeper into your face, looks, hair, body, skin, etc. I am sure the answer for most of these questions is no. The more "no" you have, the worse your health will be. When you don't feel love throughout your day in life, then hatred will start leaking into your life, and even your brain little by little until your thoughts change, your language changes, your behavior changes as well—all avoiding and hating this person or place or occasion or even yourself.

You will feel that your heart is no longer beating with love. It only beats for your empty body just to live. And here, anxiety starts because you start thinking that what is going within you is going with everybody that is surrounding you, the job that you work in, your colleagues that you're working with, your neighbors. Basically, you will see it in every detail in your life. So please love and love and feel the love, because what goes around comes around.

Letting go of the victim's mind

Letting go of the victim mindset is crucial. One of the most effective methods is releasing the victim mentality and taking control of your own life.

When you perceive yourself as a victim, you empower anything or anyone, even any situation, to dictate your destiny and actions. This implies that you lack the power to navigate through challenging situations. It's essential to recognize, deep in your heart, that you are solely responsible for your past, your present moment, and even your future. This doesn't mean exerting control and stressing to make things align with your expectations. It's about taking responsibility for the outcomes, reactions, and your responses to any situation you encounter.

Understanding the distinction between trying to control a situation and taking responsibility for your own life is significant. The former works against you, while the latter works for your best interests. You can grasp this difference by learning to accept each situation, believing that everything unfolds for your benefit. Though it might not be easy initially, keep telling yourself, "I know this is for my best," and with time, you'll witness it. The duration can vary from minutes to years, but always remember, it's for your best.

On the flip side, attempting to control every aspect of your life, thinking it will lead to better circumstances, only adds unnecessary pressure. It's like swimming against the current. Relax, let go, and understand how easy and convenient it is to allow yourself to flow with the natural course of life.

Each time you recall or dwell on a situation or someone who has caused you pain, and when you discuss how difficult it was, you are inadvertently granting more power to that situation and person. This power, however, works against you. Describing the hardship of a situation signals to yourself that you can be easily overcome.

By adopting a victim mentality, you indirectly convey to yourself, "I am not strong enough, I am not good enough, I cannot handle it myself." This significantly undermines the self-esteem you should possess. Gradually, you may find yourself resembling a fragile glass board ready to shatter with the slightest breeze on a sunny day. Fears and anxiety surround you.

Yet, you have the ability to transform this mental state into immense power. The key is a simple shift in mindset. Whenever you think about the difficulties of a particular situation, affirm, "I know I am capable of dealing with it." And indeed, you will.

No matter how challenging or painful a situation may be, once you convince yourself that you are capable and will handle it, your mind adopts a heroic, brave, and confident mindset. This mindset requires no external assistance and empowers you to navigate through difficulties. Label it as the hero mind, the brave mind, or the confident mind, and it will guide you out of adversity. When you affirm this to yourself, you cease dwelling on the past's hardships and focus more on a promising future.

When faced with challenging situations, the common question arises: "Why me? Why is this happening?" However, the more "why" questions you ask, the tougher the situation becomes. By questioning, you inadvertently communicate to your brain that you are a victim, draining your energy and attracting situations that perpetuate this victimhood. It's crucial to shift your thinking from "why" to acceptance, realizing that everything is fixable. This shift transforms your energy from victimhood to leadership, allowing you to take control of your life.

Once you embrace the belief that everything is fixable and within your capacity to handle, gratitude will surround you. Recognizing that the situation is here for your growth, you'll be thankful for the opportunity to discover answers that lead to progress. You don't need to know everything or the end of the story, but you'll be grateful that the situation is propelling you towards a better phase. Take one step at a time toward a brighter future, guided by the illuminated path revealed to you, much like a flashlight on the steps ahead.

Go back to your instincts

When I contemplated writing this book, my instinct guided me from the beginning. The more I pondered the human experience and our connection to nature from our inception, the richer information I could incorporate into this book. In challenging situations such as illness, separation, death, job loss, or financial setbacks, our initial response is to shut off logical thinking. We often succumb to stress, tears, and dwell on the difficulty of the situation, placing blame on others. However, returning to our instinct, once we calm down, allows us to discern a way out of these challenges. It enables us to understand the underlying reasons for our predicaments.

For instance, I battled anxiety and fear of nonexistent things. Upon introspection into the emotions dominating my life, I discovered a profound sense of hatred for every aspect of my existence. I had conditioned myself not to love, forgetting that love is the antithesis of fear.

To tap into this understanding, find a secluded space without interruptions, take a few deep breaths, and attain complete calmness. Pose a simple question to yourself, "What do I need to learn from this situation?" This deep calmness will unveil the answers. Practicing this step for a few days may be necessary until you hear the answer, but persistence is key. Once you grasp the answer, you'll discern your next steps or understand the purpose behind the challenges you're facing.

Your instinct holds the answers you seek, but it communicates in its own language, requiring you to learn how to interact with it. The most effective way to grasp this language is through meditation, attaining a deep level of calm that allows your instinct to articulate itself. However, be aware that this instinct communicates sparingly, usually responding with just one or a couple of direct and profound words that pinpoint the core of the issue. Prepare yourself to hear these responses and contemplate them deeply.

This lovely instinct is straightforward, and once you comprehend the meaning of the word it provides, you can uncover solutions to your problems. It reveals whether there's a breakdown in communication, issues with your personality, or challenges in your approach to things or situations. Accepting these answers is crucial for the continuation of the process; otherwise, you'll remain stuck where you are.

Strong effective affirmation

Expressing gratitude and positive affirmations can indeed be powerful for personal growth and healing. Here are some strong and effective affirmations that you can use or modify based on your needs:

1. I am grateful for the abundant healing energy flowing through my entire being.

2. Every day, my body is renewing itself with vibrant, healthy cells. Thank you, God.

3. I appreciate the uniqueness of my mind and body, a special gift from God.

4. My life is a continuous journey of relaxation and peace. Thank you, God.

5. I am thankful for the wealth and prosperity that surrounds me.

6. Gratitude fills my heart for the fulfilling career path I am on. Thank you, God.

7. My life is blessed with an incredible spouse who enriches my journey.

8. I am thankful for the warmth and comfort of my wonderful home.

9. Gratitude flows for the positive and supportive people in my life.

10. Thank you, God, for the joy and success of my amazing children.

Feel the depth of each affirmation and let it resonate within you for a more profound impact on your healing and well-being.

The list can keep going and will never end, but this is how it should be. And again, with each affirmation, try to convey as many feelings as possible, as if it's real and already exists at the right moment. Some of these affirmations even need your imagination working with them, such as the house one. So when you say that affirmation and feel it, imagine the house, providing as many details as you can – the bedrooms, the kitchen, the outside – and feel as if you are inside it, living right now. Some people tend to create a vision board, on which they can put pictures, words, or affirmations that support these goals. This could be a great idea if you'd like to have it as a reminder where you spend most of your time, even at home in a specific room or at work. You get to choose your own method of how to do it.

Forgiveness

Going through a problem in your life caused by someone else will normally make you hold onto some negative emotions within you. Each one of us is different in how strongly these emotions will affect us and how long we are going to keep them within. Of course, these emotions won't be pleasant at all. They might start with some sad feelings, guilt, or shame, but what is more dangerous is when it reaches hatred, which is, in other words, losing the ability to forgive.

Each one of us has their own story. Some stories are so sad and tough that you might say, "I can't leave this behind me; I am still living with this burden and I will for the rest of my life." I know. I totally understand that you were harmed. I totally understand that the harm is living inside your body and mind. I totally understand how awful it was when you went through that. But you know, it's your choice, my friend. It's your choice to keep holding the garbage bag that is so filthy and filled with all the harm that someone else caused you someday. It's your choice to keep it over your shoulders all these years and the coming ones. It's your choice to keep smelling the filthy smell that is there on your shoulders. It's your choice to keep the weight on your shoulders all these years and the coming ones as well. It's your choice to keep leaning down because of all the heavy weight that you are holding. And it's your choice to stay messy due to the garbage that will leak on you. But you know what? It's also your choice to throw it away and move ahead. Yes, just that one step, throw it away. It's your choice.

Do you know that the people who have hurt you someday might not even remember it? They might be living their lives without even giving any attention that they ever hurt you someday. They might have chosen to continue with their lives. So just leave them to their destiny.

Forgiveness is such a hard thing to be done. I know. But there are a few things that I'm going to share with you that will help because I know how filthy and smelly this garbage bag is. Some people have some close relationship to it as if they became friends. So here are some steps that will help you think clearly and take this action.

1. You are not an angel yourself. It's not your job to judge people. They had to do it since it's part of your journey.

2. You have no idea how life is going for them. Pray for them. You need to heal. Healing means cleaning your soul and body.

3. There's a huge difference between the person who did the harm and the harm itself, so only judge the action that was taken towards you. By looking at the action itself and seeing the difference between the person and the action, you will actually find it easier to forgive.

Don't take it too seriously

Don't take it too seriously; laugh about the fact that you've ever had a panic attack or still have them. Find humor in the feelings that come with it, make jokes about how your brain and body react during these episodes. By making it look funny and even silly, you won't make the attack pass easier or faster, but taking it too seriously can magnify the feeling. When you sense the symptoms of a panic attack, just laugh and say, "Oh, I'm having one now." Treat it as a joke to signal your brain that it's okay and even fun to have one, helping your emotions settle. If it doesn't work the first time, it will in the next one. Keep the commitment to joke about it and make it seem silly. Remember, to reach the other end of the river, you must do the work daily. The more you do it, the better and faster results you'll achieve. Some days may feel challenging, and that's okay; you're human. Just keep trying, and the more you try, the easier it gets. As your brain and body were trained to be anxious at some point in your life, they can now be trained to be relaxed and released.

Change your story

Yes, just stop talking about it. Stop sharing your old story with everyone. Ignore it completely, as if it never happened. Don't mention it anymore. Live a new day and a new life with a fresh story, as if it was never part of your life. By doing that, you are creating a new present and future for yourself without even noticing. You don't have to force yourself to forget or suppress your thoughts about it. All you need to do is create new things and stories, a new present that has nothing to do with this old past. Easily achieve this by engaging in new activities like going out with friends, participating in group exercises, dedicating time to a hobby you enjoy, or exploring a different job. Fill your time with different things that are unrelated to the old life that used to remind you of your circumstances.

I understand that this might not be as easy as it seems, but just like every rule and every lesson, the more you do it, the faster it gets. There will be times when you might feel down, hopeless, or even depressed, and that is completely fine. Tomorrow is a new day, a new story, and a new challenge. Keep trying and believe that this can be achieved.

I'm halfway there

I am halfway or almost there. This is a very important and dangerous stage that you need to be aware of. You need to study it first to be ready for it in your healing journey when it appears. I see that everyone who chooses to commit to healing will have to reach this point. I'm not talking about some people who try for one or a few days and then quit again. I am talking about the people who will keep trying as hard as they can to reach healing. But some of those people do it to the end, and some don't, and here I will explain why.

When a person suffering from anxiety or panic attacks starts to go through the healing path, doing all the effort that can be done, either by fixing the diet, meditation, affirmations, etc., there will be days that this person will start to feel better. Life will look better. The emotions will be calmer. But at the same time, little after these glory days, there will come back some of the negative emotions and feelings, and of course, thoughts that will set this person back. These times can be as bad as this person might feel as if he had made no progress at all. These negative emotions will rain again after a sunny week. So in this stage, the human brain will be in a fight to see which path you will end up taking. Is it the path to the old habits and thoughts and emotions, or is it the new path of the new thoughts and habits?

The old path looks more familiar and clearer to the brain; the brain knows it and knows every detail of it and won't be lost in it. On the other hand, the other path looks dark, and the brain doesn't know it yet. I want you to imagine it like that. You are moving forward with your new thoughts, but the brain is chaining them with some rubber chains. The more you move with your new thoughts into the new path, the more you will pull the rubber chains. The chains will tighten your thoughts more with every pull you do, bringing you back to the old thoughts. The tension forming in these rubber chains is exactly the stage that I'm talking about.

So here, it's your decision. It's either you choose to be weaker than the rubber chains and relax to go back to your old path with all its thoughts and feelings that you are used to. Or choose to be stronger than the rubber chains and make this last step ahead, cutting these rubber chains forever, ending all your old paths. Even though it will be challenging, it will cut and give you a big push to the new path. Here, the other chain of your old behavior and thoughts will have no power over you anymore. You are free from it. That is the reason I'd just explain why this stage is a very critical one because most people tend to relax back into their old path. This stage is one of the hardest stages in the healing journey. It might be painful, full of fear, hard, or even seem impossible to cope with. Because when a person starts to see and feel the healing, at this point, the body is so thirsty to feel good. The mind is in tension, so it will feel great to feel a sense of relief somehow. The majority of people won't get the idea and won't stand the fact that their body and mind are going back to feel these negative feelings on the setback. That's why the setback can look tough and hard to go through. But the fact is that it is just like the old feeling that the person was experiencing someday. The person loves to feel relief.

There are some physical and mental things that will show up in this stage:

1. You will feel more energetic.

2. You will have a longer relaxing time.

3. You will do things that used to scare you, but this time without worrying ahead of time. After doing it or while doing it, you will notice that you did not worry about it.

4. If you are using positive affirmations, your brain will start using them more often and without the effort that you used before, as if it is your normal way to live.

5. You will feel you are closer to healing, although you still don't feel great.

6. You might wake up suddenly in a very big rush of negative thoughts and emotions out of nowhere, with the feeling that you lost it all. Don't worry, remember there are only a few more steps left in your healing journey and you will reach there, feeling proud of what you have accomplished. Keep up the hard work because it is a little more, and things will be much easier.

Don't name it

Studies show that many people, throughout their lives, have cancer without knowing it, as their bodies naturally heal from it without any treatment effort. On the other hand, if a person is informed by a doctor after certain tests that they have cancer, the mental state will shift into fear, rejection, pain, or even playing the role of a victim. These high waves of negative emotions can cause the body to retain these cancer cells and may even increase them, hindering the body's natural healing. However, when a sick person receives mental support along with physical support, the chance of reaching a healing state is much higher.

If you ask me about the connection between anxiety and cancer, I'll tell you it's exactly the same. Naming your illness or the phase your brain and mind are going through gives that illness or mental problem high power, as if it is telling you, "I do exist in you." Naming assures you that you are dealing with it and need to expend effort from now on to address or eliminate it. The more you try to push things away, the more they stick closer to you by the law of attraction, as there's now a thought in the brain, a feeling in the body, and physical action taken to deal with it. Essentially, you are dealing with anxiety with all your power.

Take action

Taking action is essential for personal progress. Achieving goals or even taking small steps daily contributes significantly to the meaning of one's life. Living with goals, no matter how modest, helps break the anxious loop of thoughts and actions. It redirects attention towards more meaningful aspects of life. In my opinion, setting goals that differ from those focused on escaping anxiety is crucial. Instead of actions driven by fear avoidance, try taking actions and setting goals towards achieving something. This is vital because if the goal is merely to escape anxiety, it tends to linger closer. For instance, if you have anxiety and struggle to leave the house, set a goal to walk for a few minutes in your neighborhood for enjoyment and fresh air. However, if the goal is framed as "I need to walk to avoid thinking about my fears," your fears may accompany you on the walk.

Living your life day by day on this path can transform your entire life, changing your attitude towards yourself, loved ones, kids, and your job. Apply this approach to every aspect of your life. When setting any goal, take the path directly to it, not the one running away from pain and fears. For instance, if you dislike your job or have an unpleasant boss, your goal should be to enjoy your job to the fullest each day, not just to finish with fewer headaches or problems. Work towards adding fun to your work atmosphere, perhaps by smiling, engaging with colleagues positively, or introducing enjoyable changes. Strive to be the best in your job, improving each day, and enhancing your work environment.

If you approach work with the attitude of 'I can't wait until my shift is done,' trying to escape, you add more pressure and anxiety. Instead, enjoy your day with the abilities available to you. Start now to move towards the best in your life for healing and achieving your goals. Even if you're unsure of your goals, set simple ones achievable in a day. For example, if you're a housewife, set a goal to exercise for 30 to 45 minutes today. Commit to it, as a goal requires effort. Understand that things might be challenging at the beginning, and that's okay. Keep trying, practicing, and don't stop.

Believing

People with anxiety disorders often feel they can't control their body and mind when faced with anxious situations, but it's essential to recognize that control is a choice. When going through the anxious cycle, firmly declare, "Enough, I am the controller now." Some may argue that they've tried this without success, but the key lies in unwavering belief and continuous belief in one's ability to take control.

Belief, in its deeper sense, involves visualizing the final result of what you are moving toward, be it healing or any other goal, particularly mental healing in this case. Complete belief sends signals to your body and mind that the healing already exists, requiring consistent effort on every level to manifest. The stronger your belief, the faster you will reach your goal. When you set your mind to have complete faith in a certain goal, you can see it even before it happens. Once you believe, it is achieved. Your words and behavior must align with this belief, making it a crucial aspect of the believing step. For instance, if you believe in achieving mental healing, avoid saying, 'I'm in the worst days of my life'; instead, choose words that match your belief, such as, 'I'm mentally and emotionally stable'. Be mindful of your thoughts and words consistently.

Start noticing your thoughts; begin observing what you say to yourself. It's all there inside. You will see miracles happening as you change your beliefs and thoughts in a positive direction. I want to show you a very simple example of how powerful your beliefs and thoughts can be. Look at your face in the mirror—how does your skin look? Is it filled with imperfections? Or do you know anybody close to you who has them? If you do, have you ever noticed that these only exist on your face, and the rest of your body, such as your hands, belly, or legs, is clear? Why is that? Simply because what you focus on will grow, and what you believe in will manifest. If you are focusing on how bad your face looks, then it becomes even worse. But you never say, "Look how bad the skin on my stomach is," so it always stays clear. Be aware of your thoughts and the beliefs deep within you. Change them in a way that works for your best.

Choose to be healthy

Health is a decision, 100% a decision.

The human body is clever and unique, responding precisely to your commands. You might argue, "I didn't tell my body to become sick or ill." Sorry to say, but yes, you did. You kept affirming it until your body listened and followed your instructions.

How does this happen? A person with a low understanding of life experiences and events tends to react in ways that don't serve them well. When faced with an unfamiliar or challenging situation, they may express negative emotions like fear, hate, shame, or guilt. These emotions need an outlet, but many people don't know how to release them, unaware that they linger within the body. They remain locked down.

Each person thinks differently, attributing shame or guilt to the same situation. Specific feelings, if not released, can lead to damage and illness. By choosing your feelings, you are essentially choosing your state of health.

What should I do to stop that? You have to be neutral about all that is going on in your life. Situations in life are not good or bad; it's what you choose to think about them. By thinking in such a way, you start building your emotions. And then, by not being trained how to let go of these emotions, you, by keeping them inside, cause your body to be sick depending on the kind of emotions you had in the first place. So, by being neutral, you stop judging each situation, and you simply accept it as it is and try to deal with it showing no emotions.

You might say, but some life events and situations are so hard that we can't be neutral, such as the death of loved ones. That is true; in such cases, you should feel the sadness for a few days, accept the situation, and choose directly to go on with your life. So the decision has to be made, or otherwise, you might be stuck there.

For example, if you had a situation in which you had to have someone telling you in your face how bad you are as a person, most people in such a situation will be so angry and frustrated, while they can only say 'it's their opinion' and go on with their life. This reaction needs training. You must train yourself daily that no matter what happens, nothing will affect me. This way of living and dealing with situations and circumstances will make you a bulletproof person. This means that no matter how rough or tough people or life events might be, you will keep going with your life, following your goals and dreams. When you reach this step, you will gain the ability to be emotionally stable at all times, and that is a huge achievement in your life that you need to reach to have a better life.

Crying emotions out

Crying can be a very effective way to release all those unhealthy emotions rooted within the human body and mind. When you cry, you release those feelings from the body. Imagine a balloon that you are filling with air; the balloon has a certain point at which it will explode. But if you fill this balloon little by little, imagine it being released, and all the air inside escapes. The human body and mind are exactly like this balloon, so when you cry, you release those emotions.

Tears also wash away all this pain. However, keep in mind that when you cry, you need to have the intention to release these emotions. I mean that you don't want to cry just about how awful you are feeling; instead, you need to cry to get rid of and release those negative emotions. Each time you cry, you release the negative emotions little by little. Depending on the life situation you are facing, you might discover the need to cry out emotions you never knew existed inside. For example, you might initially feel sad, but after crying a few times, you might sense deep-seated anger within you that was buried in your mind and soul, unnoticed. Work on yourself in different ways to let go of this anger.

I'm not saying anger or any other feeling is inherently good or bad; I'm suggesting you may need to give yourself the opportunity to express it. Figure out the best way for your body, soul, and self to get rid of these emotions. Some find crying to be a healthy and effective way to release emotions, while others may feel that screaming, hitting a punching bag, or hugging a pillow works better for them. The idea is that pain arises when you keep those emotions inside. You need to release this pain, bring it to the surface, and let it go. The only person who can help you with that story is yourself.

Some people may feel better from the first day they cry, even within the first five minutes. Others may take longer, depending on how painful, strong, and deep those emotions are buried within their mind and soul. Even if someone initially feels better, they might experience the pain again after a few days, indicating that other painful emotions are resurfacing. They must cry them out or find their way to release them. Once released from these emotions, they will feel the relief, and things will start to look different for them.

This process requires effort, it's not as simple as it seems. Take time to reflect on what truly matters to you. Consider what's happening in your mind and life, focusing on things that bother you, make you sad, or evoke negative emotions. Identify these thoughts and aspects causing discomfort, and then work on addressing them one by one. Don't rush; persist until you experience complete release and relief, altering your perspective and actions. When you free yourself from this sadness, it reflects in your expression. Sadness manifests in the eyes, even if hidden, but releasing it through crying transforms your face and eyes, making them shine with a newfound glow.

Change your thoughts about it

Each person experiencing an anxiety disorder must delve deep into their mind to uncover the root cause triggering this anxiety. Some individuals navigate life unaware of the primary reason behind their anxious thoughts, while others immediately recognize the source. Whether it's a person, action, place, or specific type of food, the potential reasons are numerous. To comprehend this initial phase of the healing process, each individual must identify the precise source of their fear or anxious thoughts, retracing to the very beginning of what caused these feelings.

For instance, consider someone who experiences heightened anxiety whenever a specific person comes to mind or is encountered. This suggests that the individual causing anxiety has influenced their thinking in a way that triggers anxious feelings. To address this, one should reassess the significance of the person: Are they truly important? Do they hold power over your life? Is their presence indispensable for a better life and future? By asking such questions, you redirect your thoughts, prompting your brain to explore different perspectives on the relationship. As the brain seeks alternative answers, your perception of this person can undergo a significant shift within seconds, minutes, hours, or even days. Reflecting on your innate freedom since birth reinforces the realization that no one else has control over you. You can liberate yourself from self-imposed thoughts about the power this person holds over you. Anxiety in relationships often arises when individuals perceive a need for internal change but feel restricted by someone else's influence. Taking a few moments for self-reflection and engaging in a constructive inner dialogue can help dismantle the perceived power dynamics. It's crucial to recognize that, regardless of someone's wealth, strength, or influence, their attempts to control others stem from inner weakness. Reminding yourself of your inherent strength and autonomy is a simple yet powerful practice. Repeatedly affirming your self-worth and acknowledging that the other person, no matter their actions, is just one individual in the vast universe, can shift your perspective. This approach empowers you to overcome past negative experiences and prepares you to face future challenges as a more resilient and self-assured individual.

You know, there comes a point where you really don't want to remember the past. Not because it makes you sad; no, it's just because it really doesn't matter. You are what you are today. You are what you are now. You have deeply changed from within yourself, but all of that change is for your best, making you a tougher and stronger person. I know the harm you might have seen in your life was so bad that it damaged and broke you from the inside. However, the minute you realize it was all just to make you a different, stronger person, and that no one has power over you, all your anxiety will disappear. Your anxiety will simply say congratulations! You've understood it. I can set you free. Congratulations for all you have done and for all you have become. Now you can do it without me.

A panic attack will never come again if the person knows how to get it out. By understanding that a panic attack is the body's way of releasing extra negative energy within, the person can engage in activities like exercise, dancing, singing, or meditation to expel this energy regularly. With the thought in the brain that 'I will never have a panic attack again because I know how to deal with my body,' the person sets the foundation. Another reinforcing thought is 'I will never have a panic attack again in my whole life because I know how to deal with my body.' Believing in these thoughts, the person can return to normal life gradually. The conviction, through repeating these simple ideas, allows everything to become true. The person can go anywhere safely without being threatened by incorrect, irrational thoughts. 'I will never have a panic attack again since I know how to handle my body.' For example, in a grocery store, even if the thought arises, I might have a panic attack, just flip the page and affirm that it won't happen, ignore it, and continue with what you are doing.

I understand that it might not work immediately, but success depends on how strongly you believe in what you tell yourself. The more you believe in it, the faster and better results you'll see. A person can't spend their entire life having panic attacks or fearing them. Conversely, a person can avoid panic attacks altogether, depending on their thoughts and lifestyle. Stressful times may come, but handling and knowing how to release stress from our minds and bodies can prevent problems. Sensing our bodies allows us to address feelings of tension, stress, fatigue, or happiness and relaxation. Starting with the idea 'I will never have a panic attack again because I know how to manage my stress,' this conviction can grow and work effectively in any situation—whether you're in a different country, traveling, on a plane, or in your car.

Convincing yourself of this idea, even in feared places, gradually builds confidence. Take small steps, like walking on your neighborhood street, then gradually adding more locations. If you start feeling fear or the possibility of a panic attack, remind yourself that you won't have one because you know how to handle stress. Keep practicing these steps, and you'll see positive changes. Remember, all the steps we've discussed work together as a package for faster healing and change.

Who said so?

Who said that you will keep living with your anxiety? As you change your mind to act upon anxiety, you can bring it back to act upon relaxation. When you have anxious thoughts about anything, you've been training your brain that you have to be anxious about it over and over again until it becomes a behavior that you take without even thinking about it, without being conscious you're doing it for certain reasons. You started to do the anxious behavior without even asking yourself why you are doing that. So it becomes a behavior that your body just does unconsciously. But you can switch all of this back just by being conscious about the thoughts that you're adding and putting in your mind. So if there is any certain action that you are anxious to do or every time you do it you're always anxious and have anxiety towards it, all you need to do is ask yourself, "Why am I anxious about it? Why am I still anxious about this activity that I'm going to do? Is there any certain reason? Is there any real reason that I need to be anxious about it?" When you start asking yourself all these conscious questions, you are giving your brain a different way of thinking. And this way needs to be dug deeper and deeper, and every time you take it, you give it more power to be there in your mind. When you start being conscious about your behaviors, you will change them because they make no sense to keep doing them. For example, if you've been spending years being anxious about going to a certain place, all you need to do is ask yourself, 'Why am I anxious about going to this place? Is there any real danger over there? Am I just doing it because I am used to doing that?' Ask yourself those questions, answer them, and give yourself the answers that really make sense. And then try to go to this place and see how you will be acting. With time you will notice that your anxiety is going less and less. Practice not being anxious; practice being relaxed going to that place.

Do you remember the feeling when your body used to shake with happiness? Do you recall the joy of listening to a song that resonated deep within you, releasing a rush of happy hormones? Can you reminisce about the excitement over an upcoming event, a dress to wear, or acquiring an object you desired? Remember the relaxation and happiness when anticipation peaked? The effect of looking at the stars or witnessing the sunset, noticing the sky's colors, brought contentment. These positive sensations stem from a body filled with positive energy, allowing you to cherish simple moments - a song, a phone call, a modest purchase. Each of us cherishes those light moments, feeling as carefree as a butterfly in the sun. You believed anything was possible, able to love and embrace life's potential. Do you recall those feelings?

When that feeling fades, or it becomes challenging to find joy in the simple things, you sense a heavy load of negative energy within. To regain balance, you must choose a way to release it, or it will dissipate on its own. Negative energy feels burdensome, convincing you that nothing is achievable, creating obstacles in your path. Just as you must step over a block at your door, you need to rise above this negative energy to move forward. Trying to progress without addressing it may lead to stumbling and falling. It's more effective to remove the block, just as removing negative energy allows you to feel lighter, opening doors to new experiences.

Find a new path (laughter)

As I explained before, when the body finds its way to release negative energy through a panic attack, it becomes accustomed to it. Consequently, it repeats this process each time the body needs relief. Similarly, if a person discovers a way to laugh and expel negative energy through laughter, the human brain, though connected and separated in various areas, operates as a cohesive unit and efficient machine. Negative energy resides within the body and must find a way out, regardless of the method. Laughing is one such way for the body to release this negativity because laughter induces a shake in the body. The stronger and more frequent the shake, the faster and easier the energy is released.

Even when someone is sad, laughter may occur, as a person might find humor in the dire situation. This happens when laughter becomes a habitual method for releasing energy. Consider the alternative: releasing energy through a panic attack. It's up to you, but the key point is that once the brain and body find a path through laughter, they tend to use it more frequently. This routine becomes ingrained, happening effortlessly without forcing the body and brain.

Mental health, like anything else, requires practice. Just as you practice other activities, you need to practice this path. You might be surprised by how quickly it becomes a natural response. Despite depression, anxiety, or challenging situations, laughter is not opposed to you; it works with you. When a person is deeply depressed or anxious, laughter becomes an even more crucial tool to release the accumulated negative energy. Take the first step, and your body will pave the way for a smoother journey every time you need it. Imagine a muddy slide you're sitting on top of. The first time you slide down, your body carves a path, making it easier for subsequent use. The same principle applies to finding your way to release energy through laughter.

With this happening, you'll notice a significant change within you. The occurrence of panic attacks will likely decrease, if not cease entirely, as the body no longer requires them to release built-up energy. The method you choose to release this energy doesn't matter; what's crucial is selecting a path that brings you happiness and relaxation.

Understanding the body's language takes time, and it might require a few attempts for both the body and mind to acknowledge that this new approach is the right one. Starting with laughter, you might still encounter a few panic attacks until your body comprehends the positive changes underway. The duration and intensity of this adjustment period depend on the severity of your case and the challenges you face. Some individuals may never experience panic attacks again, while others might encounter them briefly until their bodies fully grasp the transformative changes occurring within.

Another great benefit of using laughter as a technique for releasing extra energy from the body is that it also floods the body with mood-lifting hormones. Laughter increases the levels of happy hormones, helping individuals attain a better mood to alleviate anxiety and negative feelings. Of course, achieving optimal results requires time and patience. Essentially, it provides a dual benefit: first, expelling excess energy from the body quickly, and second, improving mood by releasing positive hormones. The effectiveness is enhanced when genuine, hearty laughs are employed. The release of happiness hormones becomes even more pronounced and influential on the body and brain, promoting a healthier life. Consider adopting this approach for a better quality of life and improved health.

You know, laughter is not the only positive path that could be taken. There are many right paths that should be taken to help you out through what is going on with you. I did explain that you can exercise, draw, dance, sing—there are many, many, many ways that could be used, but you have to keep using them until your body gets used to them.

You know, the body finds it easier to take a path that it is used to taking. Just like a baby that you are teaching to do something, when the child is being taught a certain rule or a certain way of doing things, then the child will do it every time. But if you add a change that the child doesn't really know, then the child will just do it the way he is used to until he understands the new way that things should be done.

It's much better if the information was given completely the right way from the first time. It might be easier, and the results might be faster, but in case that information was given already, a change should be added and just keep repeated every time until the body and mind dig this path deeper until it just slips all the way over it without even giving any force to do that.

Conclusion

This entire healing process works as a cohesive unit. What I mean is, you can't complete one aspect entirely and neglect the others, or selectively incorporate practices that align with your lifestyle, leaving some behind. It's an integrated process that requires addressing all facets. Strive to excel in every area, persist in your efforts until you achieve results. Form a definitive image in your mind that signals the end of your health problems. Maintain this mental image, ensuring a resolution. This mindset guarantees healing, regardless of the duration or difficulty. When you convince your brain of an endpoint, your body cells collaborate to follow the path leading to that conclusion—an essential point to bear in mind. If someone is uncertain despite taking the right actions, the brain may waver, complicating the process. A clear conclusion aids the brain's swift adjustment, guiding the body in the right direction. Those who successfully healed envisioned the healing process, firmly believing in its outcome.

Once you commit to initiating the healing process, commence immediately by addressing everything simultaneously. It's not as challenging as it sounds; in fact, it streamlines the process and accelerates positive outcomes. Opt for a healthy lifestyle, incorporating nutritious food, a balanced diet, and regular exercise. Exercise until you reach the point of sweating, while simultaneously improving your diet—less processed food, more raw ingredients, and reduced sugar intake. Allocate time daily for meditation or relaxation, providing your mind with a moment of tranquility. This routine, coupled with a healthy body, minimizes stress and anxiety, enhancing the quality of meditation. As you become more relaxed, your exercise performance improves, releasing endorphins that energize your day. Physical fatigue and reduced stress from exercise contribute to better sleep quality, creating a positive chain reaction. Each component complements the others, making it easier to incorporate additional activities that bring joy and enhance your well-being.

To embark on your healing journey, make a decisive commitment to commence the process. This clarity ensures readiness to face any challenges that may arise. Your mindset should firmly declare, "No matter what, I will persist in doing what is right."

www.ingramcontent.com/pod-product-compliance
Lightning Source LLC
Chambersburg PA
CBHW081635040426
42449CB00014B/3323